Beautiful
LAKE DISTRICT

Val Corbett

MYRIAD

LONDON

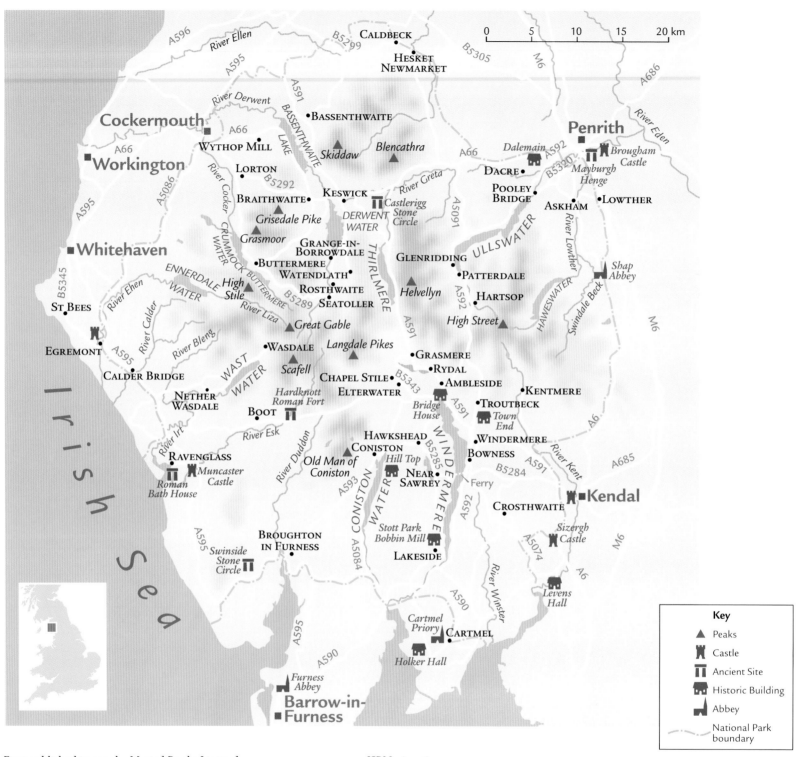

Key

▲ Peaks
♜ Castle
Ⅲ Ancient Site
🏛 Historic Building
⛪ Abbey
— · — National Park boundary

First published in 2007 by Myriad Books Limited,
35 Bishopsthorpe Road, London SE26 4PA

ISBN 1 84746 010 0
EAN 978 1 84746 010 3

Photographs and text copyright © Val Corbett

Designed by Jerry Goldie Graphic Design
Printed in China

www.myriadbooks.com

Title page: Borrowdale; right: Scafell and Wast Water

Contents

Central Lake District

The heart of the Lake District contains many of the important towns of the region such as Windermere, Bowness and Ambleside. Its stunning scenery has been a source of wonder and inspiration to artists and writers over the generations. William Wordsworth went to school in Hawkshead and spent most of his adult life at Grasmere and Rydal Mount. Pretty villages such as Hawkshead, Chapel Stile and Grasmere abound and close at hand is the Langdale valley with its unusual rock-topped "pikes".

Windermere

Many visitors catch their first view of the Lake District as they drive over the crest of the hill on the road from Kendal. Windermere is the first stretch of water they encounter and the lively town of the same name makes the perfect base for exploring the area. The 11 mile (18km) length of the lake bustles with the comings and goings of small boats and pleasure craft including the *Osprey* (above). Built in 1902, it is one of the historic wooden pleasure cruisers which ply the lake.

Windermere views

The month of September is perfect for enjoying the drifting beauty of the autumn mist that lies over the lakes. The view (above) looks south over Windermere and was taken at dawn from the lower slopes of Loughrigg Fell. Windermere is the longest of all the lakes in the Lake District, and the largest lake in England.

Windermere is the only town in the Lake District fully accessible by rail – in fact, the town developed thanks to the construction of the railway line which was built in 1848.

Just off the main road, Queen Adelaide's Hill (right), on the eastern shore of the lake, gives wonderful views of Windermere and surrounding fells. Queen Adelaide's Hill is one of the national park's seven official viewpoints in the Lakes. The idea for the viewpoints came from Thomas West, who published the first official guidebook to the Lake District in 1778. He described the scenery from a number of viewing points or "stations" which became fashionable places for visitors and artists to gather.

Bowness

Once a separate village, Bowness is now connected to the town of Windermere. This bustling settlement is one of the Lake District's tourist hotspots but it retains a great deal of its original charm. Many of the Victorian mansions built by wealthy industrialists from Lancashire in the 19th century still survive as hotels.

The lakefront with its traditional ticket offices, flowerbeds, ducks and swans retains much of the flavour of a Victorian resort despite the hustle and bustle of a modern-day tourist town. It is the perfect vantage point from which to enjoy an endless display of boats manoeuvring in and out of the bay.

Blackwell

One of Britain's most important Arts & Crafts houses lies just a mile south of Bowness. The house (above) occupies a stunning position overlooking Windermere and was designed as a holiday home by MH Baillie Scott for the Manchester brewer Sir Edward Holt. Baillie Scott who, along with John Ruskin and William Morris, was one of the major exponents of the Arts & Crafts movement of the late 19th century, built the house in the Manorial Style promoted by William Morris. Today the beautifully restored house is open to the public and contains an impressive collection of furniture, paintings, sculpture and ceramics from the period.

Bowness ferries

The village of Bowness is the centre of boating activity on England's busiest lake. The landing stage is a regular stop for passenger craft running from Lakeside at the southern end of Windermere to Waterhead at the northern end. A shuttle service carries walkers and cyclists from Bowness Bay to the quieter farther shore and connects with a minibus service to Hawkshead and beyond. A car ferry (pictured left) crosses the lake at its narrowest point between Ferry Nab and the far shore; it is the Lake District's only car ferry and runs on underwater cables.

Around Bowness

Ferries have criss-crossed Windermere for more than 500 years. In the early days passengers were even expected to help row the boats. About half a dozen small islands are scattered along the length of the lake, adding to its charm. Opposite Bowness Bay are two of the larger islands which almost cut the lake in two – Belle Isle, with its unusual round tower (built in 1774) is particularly attractive. Half a mile north of Bowness is the Windermere Steamboat Museum which has Victorian and Edwardian steamboats as well as *Esperance*, the boat made famous by Arthur Ransome in his famous children's book *Swallows and Amazons*.

In the summer Bowness is full of activities to entertain visitors. The Old Laundry Visitor Centre is home to the World of Beatrix Potter, celebrating all aspects of the writer's life. North of Windermere is the National Park Visitor Centre at Brockhole; its beautiful lakeside garden has superb views.

Troutbeck

The village of Troutbeck stretches for more than a mile along a side road off the Kirkstone Pass that links Windermere and Ullswater. It contains many wonderful examples of attractive Lake District architecture including pubs and pretty stone cottages. The famous Townend House (owned by the National Trust) is at the southern end of the village. A good example of a wealthy farmer's house, it dates from the 17th century. The village church, unusually just called "Jesus Christ", has a window by Burne-Jones and a churchyard filled with a cheery mass of daffodils in spring.

For many years Troutbeck was the centre of the greatest of the annual hound-trailing meetings held throughout the Lake District. The hounds pursued a pre-laid scent up the peaks through torrents and over drystone walls. Thousands of spectators would descend on Troutbeck from all over Cumbria.

Ambleside

Surrounded by beautiful mountain scenery, Ambleside lies on the main road that runs between Keswick and Kendal. Much more than a village – it even has its own cinema – Ambleside has a thriving student community at St Martin's College, and hosts the Lake District summer music festival. The oldest part of the town, the route up to the Kirkstone Pass, has some attractive old houses and streets. Peggy Hill, off North Road and sharply up hill from Stock Bridge, is a good place to start.

Dating from the 17th century, Bridge House on Rydal Road (below) is a National Trust property. Originally a summer house for Ambleside Hall, the building straddles Stock Beck. Beyond it are the old mill buildings complete with waterwheel, which are now a restaurant. In the mid 19th century this tiny building was home to the Rigg family – mother, father and six children. In 1926 the house was purchased by local people for a sum of £450 and donated to the National Trust who used it as their first information office.

Ambleside views

The village of Ambleside developed next to Stock Beck, whose fast-flowing waters powered the local watermills. Traces of this history can be seen all around the town. The Water Wheel Shop (left) is a converted mill and still has an intact waterwheel on the outside of the building together with some pieces of machinery inside.

The commanding 180ft (55m) spire of St Mary's Church dominates the town. The church was built in 1854 to a design by Sir George Gilbert Scott, the architect made famous by his London buildings including St Pancras station and the Albert Memorial. The famous Lakeland poet William Wordsworth had his office in the town when he was distributor of stamps for Westmorland. He is commemorated, together with his wife and sister, by a memorial chapel and stained-glass window. St Mary's also boasts a handsome mural depicting the ancient rush-bearing ceremony in which parishioners once covered the church floors with fresh rushes every summer.

Waterhead attractions

The pier at Waterhead was established in 1845 at the northernmost point of Windermere. Passengers often alight at the pier surprised to find that it is almost a mile away from the town of Ambleside, which may explain why a horse-drawn carriage does good trade, carrying passengers between the ferry and the town.

Waterhead is a busy ferry terminal: steamers and launches sail all year round to Bowness and Lakeside. It is also possible to hire a rowing boat at the pier for a more leisurely exploration of the northern reaches of the lake.

Nearby, Borrans Park is a tranquil spot overlooking the lake with the remains of the important Roman fort, Galava, still visible nearby. This fort was one of a chain built by the Emperor Hadrian to protect trade routes in Cumbria. A Roman road linked Galava with the fort at Hardknott and the harbour at Ravenglass.

Rydal

Rydal is best-known for its association with William Wordsworth. Rydal Mount (far left), one of several characterful houses in the village, was the poet's home for the last four decades of his life. In contrast to the simplicity of Dove Cottage, his previous home in Grasmere, Rydal Mount was grand and spacious. The house is now open to the public and contains beautiful furniture, together with family possessions and portraits. The gardens are laid out as they were when the poet was in residence. Opposite Rydal Mount is Rydal Hall (left) an imposing 17th century house now owned by the Diocese of Carlisle and used as a conference and retreat centre. The formal gardens are open to the public with a little cafe nearby. The waterfall and viewing hut (below left) in the grounds is an idyllic spot in which to linger.

Rydal Water

One of the Lake District's smallest lakes, Rydal Water (below) lies in a sheltered bowl, and early morning mists are common. A popular walk leads around the lake hugging the western shore, before crossing the river Rothay on a high-level path that drops into Rydal village past Wordsworth's final home.

Elterwater

Four miles west of Ambleside, the much-visited little village of Elterwater is scenically placed at the entrance to the Langdale valley and shares its name with the adjacent small lake. The first view of the village, coming either from Grasmere or Ambleside, is always impressive with the Coniston Fells and Langdale Pikes forming a dramatic background. The village was formerly industrial, and its pretty little slate cottages (above) were built for the workers at the nearby slate quarries. A walking route to Little Langdale takes in views of old and new slate quarries. Later a gunpowder manufacturing business brought workers to the village. The Britannia Inn (right), with its low ceilings and slate floors, is the focal point of the village.

Elterwater is the smallest of the 16 lakes in the Lake District. "Elter" is the Norse word for swan, so Elterwater literally means "Swan Lake". Whooper swans regularly migrate to the lake in winter from Iceland.

Chapel Stile and Great Langdale

The tiny village of Chapel Stile is the kind of place where it seems perfectly normal to meet sheep walking along the middle of the village street or grazing the verge. The sturdy church, with its fortified tower, serves the whole of Langdale and is a fine sight rising above the village with Silver Howe as a backdrop. The Cumbria Way long-distance footpath enjoys the same view as it passes the village. Slate quarrying, both past and present, is evident everywhere; the scree on the fellside, the occasional boom of quarry blasting and the village houses themselves which are almost all built of slate.

Grasmere

At the very heart of the Lake District, just off the main road from Ambleside to Keswick, Grasmere is famous as the home of William Wordsworth for the most creative period of his life. The poet lived at Dove Cottage (left) and its tiny rooms are still much as they would have been when he lived there with his sister, Dorothy, and wife, Mary. The life of the poet, his family and their many visitors is brilliantly described by Dorothy in her diaries.

Looking across the lake from one of the shingle beaches on the southern shore (above) you can see the white face of the Prince of Wales Hotel on the far side. Dove Cottage is just tucked behind to the right. The view shows Helm Crag to the left, the Pass of Dunmail Raise and the soaring slopes of Seat Sandal.

Grasmere scenes

William, Dorothy and Mary Wordsworth are buried in the Church of St Oswald (above). Their gravestone (left) is a place of pilgrimage for lovers of the Lakeland poets.

The rush-bearing festival at Grasmere (below) is celebrated every August on the Saturday nearest to St Oswald's Day. It is a reminder of the time when fresh rushes were strewn each summer to keep unpaved church floors dry and fresh.

Grasmere is also home to the famous Grasmere gingerbread, which is more like a deliciously spicy shortbread than cake. It is sold from the tiny cottage on the edge of St Oswald's churchyard (below). Built in 1630, the shop was originally the village school. In 1815 Sarah Nelson, a local cook, rented the house and set herself up as a baker and confectioner. Her recipe for gingerbread became famous throughout the area and Grasmere gingerbread is still sold in the shop today.

Latterbarrow, Blea Tarn and the river Brathay

A short, sharp climb from Hawkshead leads to the summit of Latterbarrow (above) which gives dramatic panoramic views to the west across Hawkshead to the Coniston Fells. In the near distance is Blelham Tarn with the northern reaches of Windermere in the distance.

Blea Tarn (left) lies on higher ground between the two valleys of Great Langdale and Little Langdale. This bleak winter view shows the Langdale Pikes in the far distance. The waters of the river Brathay (right and overleaf) flow from Elterwater into Windermere. The Norse word "Brathay" means "broad river".

Hawkshead

Midway between Windermere and the northern end of Coniston Water, this famous village lies just north of Esthwaite Water and near the ever-popular beauty spot of Tarn Hows (left). It is a compact maze of picturesque whitewashed buildings, dominated by the church of St Michael's and All Angels (below) from its position overlooking Hawkshead.

Hawkshead is closely linked to the early of life of William Wordsworth. The poet and his brother John were both pupils at the old grammar school, founded in 1585. His desk at the grammar school, covered in carvings done by the two boys, can be seen on view in what is now a museum. As a boy, Wordsworth lodged in the cottage of Anne Tyson (right), half a mile from the village at Colthouse. Anne is reputed to have had a great influence on him: she was a gifted storyteller and may have sparked an interest in tales of the countryside in the young poet's mind.

The town also houses the Beatrix Potter Gallery, a 17th century building which was once the office of a local solicitor, William Heelis, who married the author in 1913.

Hawkeshead is picturesque, filled with colour-washed houses many with superb cottage gardens. Its arches, pillars and flights of steps set it apart from other Lakeland villages. Cars are banned from the town centre, so it is easy to imagine that you are back in the past as you walk through the higgledy-piggledy streets.

The Langdales

The Langdales consist of two valleys – Great Langdale and Little Langdale, which join at Elterwater. They are famous for dramatic and varied scenery, and are home to the rocky-topped Langdale Pikes.

The slopes around Little Langdale Tarn (above) are bathed in early morning November sun. This valley retains its traditional character, and only light traffic uses the narrow road to Wrynose Pass. The tarn itself is inaccessible by road but a popular footpath passes over the picturesque little stone Slaters Bridge which crosses the infant river Brathay soon after it leaves the tarn.

Great Langdale (right) is dominated by the Langdale Pikes which rise abruptly from the level valley floor. The area abounds in colourful names – the Pikes themselves are Pike O' Stickle and Harrison Stickle on the right, while further right is Pavey Arc, Lakeland's biggest cliff, which is cut through by Jack's Rake, a wonderfully challenging trail. Beneath is the sombrely named Dungeon Ghyll and to the left are Crinkle Crags and Bow Fell. Overleaf the view is of Great Langdale in the snow, with the Langdale Pikes in the background.

Southern Lake District

This region is a fascinating blend, from the "classic" Lakeland scenery of southern Windermere and Coniston to the pretty villages situated in lush countryside overlooking Morecambe Bay. A visit to Beatrix Potter's house at Hill Top is a must for anyone who has ever read her work and it is said that you can immediately identify the inspiration for her illustrations in the surrounding hills and fields. Coniston is packed with historical references – the Old Man looming over the town with its many disused mines, Brantwood, the lakeshore home of John Ruskin, the art critic and social reformer and the memorials to Donald Campbell who perished on the lake in an attempt to break the world water-speed record.

Near Sawrey and Esthwaite

The villages of Near and Far Sawrey lie one mile apart between Windermere and Esthwaite Water (above). Hill Top, the home of Beatrix Potter, is situated in Near Sawrey making this the better known of the two villages. The house (left) now owned by the National Trust, is open to the public. The author's furniture, china and watercolours are on display. In the kitchen garden there are delightful little tableaux, reminiscent of scenes from Peter Rabbit.

Far Sawrey is closer to Windermere and accessible on foot from the ferry. The beautifully situated St Peter's Church (right) lies across the fields from the village. It was originally built to accommodate 400 people since many of the large houses had servants.

Coniston

On a still September morning the peaks of the Old Man of Coniston and Wetherlam (left), towering above the village of Coniston, are reflected on the calm surface of Coniston Water. This view from Brantwood, the home of the critic and social reformer John Ruskin, was considered by him to be the finest in the Lake District. Further down the lake Arthur Ransome enjoyed a similar view while writing *Swallows and Amazons*.

The two views below of the village are taken in different seasons and show how the Old Man dominates the landscape above the town. The farm in the foreground, High Bank Grounds was the setting for *Swallows and Amazons*. The slopes of the slate grey mountain are scarred by the legacy of old mineworkings – copper was extracted here for more than 500 years.

Coniston views

The restored steam yacht *Gondola* (above) plies Coniston Water from the pier and calls at Brantwood. The boat combines the workmanship of a Venetian gondola with that of a Victorian steamship.

Brantwood, the home of John Ruskin, is open to the public all year round. It is perched on a narrow shelf at the foot of a steep fell high above Coniston Water. The John Ruskin museum in the town was established as a memorial to Ruskin and is a celebration of the area's heritage. The museum also honours the life of Donald Campbell whose many attempts to break the world water speed record ended in tragedy on Coniston Water. His gravestone can be seen in Coniston's new cemetery and its shape reflects his famous boat *Bluebird*.

Until the copper mines arrived in the mid 19th century, Coniston was a scattered rural community. It began to develop as a prosperous village and attracted many wealthy people who built splendid homes on the shoreline. The village is an excellent base for tourists and walkers, and boasts three pubs – the Crown, the Sun and the Black Bull. Many of the paths leaving the village take walkers past the remains of the old mineworkings and the views from the summit of the Old Man back down to Coniston Water and the village are magnificent.

Kelly Hall Tarn

This quiet stretch of water (above) lies only a short distance from the road running up the west side of Coniston Water.

The mysterious Peel Island can be glimpsed through the reeds of Coniston Water (left) at the southern end of the lake. The island features in *Swallows and Amazons* as "Wild Cat Island".

The privately-owned sculpture (right) is by the artist Anthony Gormley, famous for the Angel of the North at Gateshead.

Lakeside

One mile north of Newby Bridge, this popular spot on Windermere is busy with steam trains and pleasurecraft. The station platform and landing stages at Lakeside can be seen above the mass of hawthorn blossom on the slopes of Gummers How (left). Steam trains puff up and down the scenic little railway line which follows the river Leven for 3.5 miles from Haverthwaite. A popular way of extending the trip is to then board one of the boats run by Windermere Lake Cruises. Alternatively, in summer, a little ferry crosses the lake to Fellfoot Park and Garden, owned by the National Trust. This is the perfect spot for a picnic, a visit to the tearoom, or a wander around the Victorian gardens and along the lake shore. The Aquatarium at Lakeside is a popular choice for families – you can be nose to nose with fish and then walk in a tunnel beneath them.

Crosthwaite

In late April the Lyth and Winster valleys are awash with the white blossom of damson trees in the little orchards scattered around the area. The sheltered, warm climate of southern Lakeland is ideal for growing damsons and each spring the Westmorland damson association holds a "damson day" at Howe, near Crosthwaite. Guided walks, passing lovely old farms and orchards, are among the highlights. The fruit is made into a huge variety of products including damson gin, damson beer, chocolates and jam. The damson trees were originally planted by the monks of Furness abbey, and the skin of the fruit was used as a dye when the wool trade was at its height.

The attractive village church of St Mary's was built in 1878. The name of the village means "a cross in a clearing" which may derive from a former chapel on the same site. The church is situated next to the Punch Bowl, which dates from the 17th century.

The Church of St Mary and St Michael, Cartmel

The picturesque village of Cartmel lies two miles west of Grange-over-Sands on the southern edge of the Lake District, on a small peninsula jutting into the flat expanse of Morecambe Bay. Cartmel Priory church (above), founded in 1188, towers over the village. The priory was granted to the monks of Lindisfarne by the king of Northumbria in the 7th century. It was an ideal spot for a monastic retreat, since it was protected to the north by the mountains of the Lake District and to the south by the treacherous sands of Morecambe Bay. Although much of the priory was destroyed by Henry VIII at the time of the Dissolution of the Monasteries, the priory church and the gatehouse in the village square still survive. It is reputed to be the most beautiful church in the north-west of England. The interior of the church is vast, but rich in fascinating artefacts, which include a 200 year old umbrella, claimed to be one of the first of its kind in the world. One of the glories of the church are its beautiful stained-glass windows, which include some Pre-Raphaelite panels.

Around Cartmel

The river Eea winds its way through the village and adds charm to the side streets with their handsome houses. Cartmel Village Shop (above) on the square is the home of the famous sticky toffee pudding, a delicious but diet-defying treat! On the far edge of the village lies Cartmel racecourse which holds regular steeplechase meetings during the summer. For the rest of the year Cartmel is a sleepy and picturesque retreat.

Duddon Estuary

Located between Morecambe Bay and the west Cumbrian coast, the Duddon estuary opens into the Irish Sea just north of Barrow-in-Furness. It has a shoreline of 28 miles. The photograph above is taken from Sandale Haws nature reserve. It is on the edge of the shipbuilding town of Barrow-in-Furness but still offers views of mountains, pale sand and sky that could almost be Hebridean. Black Combe, lying across the estuary, is detached from the main Lake District mountains, but the views from its summit are hard to beat. The Coniston Fells are seen in the far distance on the right.

Harter Fell

The Duddon valley, between Coniston and Wast Water, does not contain a lake – perhaps one reason why it remains relatively unvisited. However, the river Duddon, with its rushing water, incredibly clear pools and sparkling waterfalls, is more than ample compensation. The shapely peak of Harter Fell (left) stands at the top end of the valley and is accessible from the roadside at Hardknott Pass. From the summit there are views of both the Scafell range to the north and the Coniston range to the south and east. The tiny villages of Ulpha and Seathwaite are practically the only settlements in the area.

Eastern Lake District

This area is dominated by the Helvellyn range and by two lakes, the narrow but picturesque Ullswater and the bleak Haweswater Reservoir. The high fells contain some of the Lake District's best-known mountain scenery: the steep-sided Striding Edge, Patterdale, Kirkstone Pass (Lakeland's highest mountain road) and the Roman road on High Street. The villages of Pooley Bridge and Glenridding at either end of Ullswater are ideal stopping off places for visitors wishing to explore this beautiful area.

Ullswater

Located between Pooley Bridge in the north and Glenridding in the south, Ullswater stretches for 9 miles (14.5km) and makes an elongated "z" shape giving it three separate reaches of water.

Anglers and photographers are generally the only people to be found on the shoreline of the lake, enjoying the dawn (above), where early mist, which gathers across the lake, dissolves gently as the sun rises. This view from Glencoyne looks east towards the slopes of Place Fell, with Hallin Fell beyond. The view (left) of the much-photographed boathouse near Pooley Bridge looks across to Arthur's Pike and Bonscale Pike, both good spots for a quiet fell walk.

Glencoyne Farm

The fat chimneystacks (above) are a typical feature of old lakeland farmhouses. There are two theories as to why the stacks were round: one that their shape was better for drawing smoke, the other that, "square ones are better for the devil to hide in". This view is from the path to the former miners' cottages at Seldom Seen, in Glencoynedale. It was a favourite of Queen Victoria, and in the intervening century the view remains little changed.

Wordsworth's daffodils

After walking along the Glencoyne shoreline of Ullswater (below), Dorothy Wordsworth wrote in her diary entry of 15th April 1802, "I never saw daffodils so beautiful..." William, her brother, included some of her description in his poem *I wandered lonely as a cloud*. Widely known as *Daffodils*, it is probably now the most famous poem in the English language. Because of it, many people associate the Lake District with the flower.

Patterdale

On the road between the Kirkstone Pass and Ullswater, the Patterdale valley is a mecca for mountain walkers. Towering above the small village is the Helvellyn mountain range, and one of the most popular routes to the summit lies along the skyline (left). The Coast-to-Coast long-distance footpath passes through the village, and many walkers use the excellent youth hostel.

The name "Patterdale" comes from a visit by St Patrick in the 5th century. He landed on the Duddon Sands and travelled to Ullswater, where he preached and baptised local people. The slate-built church of St Patrick in the village was erected in 1853 by the renowned Victorian architect Anthony Salvin, who also re-modelled Muncaster Castle. The church is famous for its beautiful panels dedicated to St Patrick, made by local embroiderer Anne Macbeth, a distinguished pioneer of craft education. They depict biblical scenes within the setting of Patterdale and the local area.

Glenridding

The largest village on Ullswater, Glenridding lies near the southern end of the lake on the road to the Kirkstone Pass. On weekends, when the weather is good, crowds of walkers leave Glenridding as they set off for Striding Edge. For the less ambitious, the 19th-century Ullswater steamers, *Raven* and *Lady*, will ferry you throughout the year to Howtown or Pooley Bridge.

The southern lakeshore walk from Howtown to Glenridding is reckoned to be one of the best in the Lake District, with constantly changing vistas mixed with woodland and open pasture.

The village owes its existence to the very successful leadmining at Greenside – a mine which closed as recently as the 1950s. The mine made history by being the first to instal electricity, generated by water from Keppel Cove under Helvellyn. In 1929 the reservoir at Keppel Cove burst its banks and caused devastation in the village, fortunately without casualties.

There is a national park information centre in the car park at Glenridding and inside is a recreation of a shaft of one of the Glenridding mines.

A holy well dedicated to St Patrick can be found close to the roadside, just south of the village.

Lanty's Tarn

A short, sharp climb from the main car park in Glenridding leads to the lovely, shallow Lanty's Tarn (left). This fairytale stretch of water was named after Lancelot Dobson who owned most of Grisedale. His house, just below the tarn, is now in ruins. Close by is the little knoll of Keldas. From its summit there is a wonderful view across Ullswater almost perfectly framed by Scots pine. A round walk from Glenridding to Fairfield, via St Sunday Crag and returning via Grisedale, takes you past the tarn which was built to supply water to Patterdale Hall, in the valley below. There is an ice house situated by the small dam wall. The ice was stored in a metal container, and was used during the summer by the residents of Patterdale Hall in their drinks and salads.

Striding Edge

The route up to Helvellyn is one of the most popular walks in the Lake District. In the summer there are often hundreds of walkers making their way to and from the summit. At the top, Helvellyn is grassy and remarkably flat, but at the eastern side of the fell lies the knife-sharp ridge of Striding Edge (above). The narrow path along its top has great drops on either side and can be dangerous.

Near the top of the mountain is the Gough Memorial which commemorates the death of Charles Gough, a lakeland tourist who, in 1805, died whilst trying to cross Striding Edge. His dog guarded his body for three months, before he and his master's corpse were discovered. On the left of the photograph is Red Tarn, so-called because it reflects the rosy glow of the dawn.

Kirkstone Pass

On the road between Windermere and Ullswater lies Kirkstone Pass, the highest mountain road in the Lake District. The name of the pass comes from a large boulder shaped like a church or "kirk", which lies by the side of the road. From the pass there are stunning views towards the high ground of Patterdale and over Brothers Water. In wintry weather (left) snowdrifts take on a beautifully sculptured appearance when snow is blown into the lee of the walls during blizzards.

63

Hartsop

This quiet, unspoilt village is situated in a sheltered side-valley near Brothers Water at the northern foot of Kirkstone Pass. In the past the area was busy with mining, quarrying and milling and it is worth a short walk along the track to the Hayeswater Reservoir to see the impressive ruins of the watercourse and wheel pit of the former Mires Head leadmine. On the return path to the left are the remains of a cornmill together with its grinding stones.

The village has a number of houses with first-floor spinning galleries which project into the street; these were used for the display and drying of fleeces rather than spinning wool.

Brothers Water

A short distance outside Hartsop, on the track to Patterdale and Ullswater, is this dramatic view of Brothers Water (below). Hartsop Hall, a picturesque farmhouse dating from the 16th century can be seen on the far side, sheltered by the slopes of High Hartsop Dodd. Brothers Water was previously called Broad Water but was renamed after the tragic drowning of two brothers in the 19th century.

Angle Tarn

Not to be confused with the stretch of water of the same name under Bowfell, Angle Tarn lies high above Patterdale and Hartsop. The tarn has a gentler appearance than many other high level lakes since it is attractively cupped by surrounding crags and is unusually indented and reedy. In the far distance are the more northerly stretches of the Helvellyn range. The route of the coast-to-coast walk passes close by.

Haweswater and High Street

This stretch of water (above and right) is a reservoir created in the 1930s. It has a peaceful air, but submerged beneath the water lies the old village of Mardale, drowned when the valley was flooded. A wall runs intermittently along the 28 mile length of High Street (left), the course of a Roman road.

Askham

Described by the famous fell-walker and writer Alfred Wainwright as "the most attractive village in Westmorland", Askham lies five miles south of Penrith on the road to Haweswater. The pretty cottages line an unusually long and wide village green. The road through the village climbs steadily for nearly a mile from Askham church, by the bridge over the river Lowther, to the gateway of Askham Fell. Most of the cottages were built towards the end of the 17th century and many have impressive datestones.

Around the village

Askham boasts two historic pubs – the 17th-century Queen's Head, with wooden beams, and the 18th century Punch Bowl on the village green. The Punch Bowl was once a watering hole for travellers on their way to the village of Mardale, the village which disappeared when the reservoir at Haweswater was built. At the lower end of the village lies Askham Hall, the family home of Lord Lonsdale. The hall is a mainly Tudor addition to an early defensive pele tower. A short distance from the village is St Peter's Church, built in 1832 and funded by the Earl of Lonsdale, the original owner of Askham Hall. The

ruins of Lowther Castle are just across the river – the towers can be seen from the village, rising above woodland. Once the entire village was part of the Lowther Estate.

Unusually, one of Askham's main attractions today is a heated outdoor swimming pool. Open from June to the middle of September, it is run by the local community.

Lowther

Situated five miles south of Penrith in beautiful parkland on the eastern fringes of the Lake District lies the spectacular Gothic ruin of Lowther Castle. The estate villages of Lowther New Town and Lowther village lie about half a mile from the castle and church. The castle was built in 1810 for the Lowther family,

influential landowners who lived at nearby Askham Hall. The "Yellow Earl", the fifth Lord Lonsdale (1880-1944), was a great character but notoriously extravagant. He hired more than 90 staff for the castle. This high-spending lifestyle eventually led to the castle's decline; there are now plans to restore it.

Pooley Bridge

This bustling village lies close to the northern tip of Ullswater, where the river Eamont leaves the lake, about five miles south of Penrith. Until recently Pooley Bridge was a quiet backwater; now it bustles with visitors and sometimes feels as if it is in danger of being swamped. The narrowness of the old bridge, built for horses and carts, causes occasional log jams as cars try to cross at the height of the summer. King John granted the fishing village its charter in the 12th century. On the market square stands an unusual millennium monument consisting of a sandstone pillar topped by a weather vane and a fish. From the village there are walks up onto Moor Divock, an area rich in prehistoric remains which include the ancient Cockpit stone circle.

The Ullswater Steamer Company boats link Pooley Bridge with Howtown and Glenridding and connect with excellent walks on the eastern side of the lake.

Dacre

This small village of pretty cottages, with its ancient moated castle (right), fascinating church and good pub, lies on a minor road leading from the A66 to Ullswater, six miles south-west of Penrith. Dacre Castle was originally one of the 14th century pele towers, built to defend the English border against the Scottish reivers. The castle has walls 7ft thick and 66ft high; the first floor consists of one single enormous room with a trussed roof and fireplaces on opposite walls. It is known as "the room of the three kings" as it is believed that two Scottish kings and the king of Cumberland met here to sign a peace treaty. The castle has been carefully restored into a dramatic residence.

The Church of St Andrew's

This Norman church is beautifully cared for by its parishioners. A large stone bear marks each corner of the churchyard. The bears appear to tell the story of a small cat or lynx which jumps onto the bear's back; eventually the bear fights off its tormentor, eats the cat and falls into a contented sleep. Beyond this the origins of the bears and their significance is a puzzle. Inside the church there are many monuments to the Hassell family of Dalemain, the original owners of Dacre Castle, including a superb modern window. Another modern window commemorates Willie Whitelaw, the Conservative politician who is buried at the church. On the floor is an engraved stone, thought to be a Viking grave. One mile from Dacre lies the stately home of Dalemain, with its famous garden, which was bought by Sir Edward Hassell in 1769.

Northern Lake District

Keswick, the largest town in the Lake District, and its adjoining lake of Derwent Water with its stunning scenery and boating attractions make this easily the most popular destination for visitors to the Northern Lakes. But this area is packed with many other scenic treasures. Bassenthwaite and the three adjoining lakes of Buttermere, Crummock Water and Loweswater are all surrounded by stunning fells with a scattering of characterful and pretty villages. Literary and historic associations abound, particularly in the remote valleys of Borrowdale and Buttermere.

Keswick

In a superb position, backed by Skiddaw and overlooking Derwent Water and the north Lakeland fells, Keswick plays host to a large number of visitors throughout the year. The town is the undisputed hub of the northern Lake District and is an ideal stopping off point for those visiting the northern lakes. Keswick's industrial origins as a mining town are now largely forgotten, but it retains many interesting buildings connected with its history. In 2001 the cricket ground in Fitz Park (above), with its splendid backdrop of Skiddaw, won the Wisden accolade of "the most beautiful ground in Britain".

Around Keswick

The Moot Hall, which dates from 1813, is Keswick's best known landmark. It houses the tourist information centre and, at its west end, is the famous "one-handed clock". In the past the hall served as a courthouse, a museum, a prison and a local market. The bell in the tower bears the date 1601 and the letters HDRO. It is thought that this came from the ancestral home of the Derwentwater family on Lord's Isle.

From the boat landings it is possible to hire a rowing boat (right) or take one of the many pleasure trips around the lake. There are splendid views of Cat Bells, Skiddaw and the many islands that grace Derwent Water including St Herbert's Island and Lord's Island, both of which are owned by the National Trust.

Derwent Water

Located beneath the fells of Cat Bells and Skiddaw, Derwent Water is one of the larger of the lakes in the region – at its widest point it is just over a mile wide. Seen at dawn (top left) this view from Friar's Crag across to Borrowdale was a favourite of John Ruskin. Visitors can enjoy it by taking a short stroll past Keswick's landing stages. The little hill of Castlehead, close to Keswick, provides a view (top right) to the west towards Cat Bells and Causey Pike. The view (left) is from the peak of Cat Bells with the massive bulk of Skiddaw and Blencathra looming behind Keswick.

Derwent Water sunset

The first snows of winter coat the summit of Skiddaw seen here in the distance across Derwent Water. To the right is the Ashness launch landing stage, one of seven on the lake. The traditional teak launches operate a frequent service, useful to walkers since the 12 mile (19km) circuit can be too much for the casual visitor.

Ashness Bridge

Taken on a morning in February, ice has formed on the rocks of Barrow Beck which flows under this ancient packhorse bridge on the road to Watendlath. This is one of the Lake District's treasured views and is photographed by literally thousands of people every year. From here the lake is only visible in the far distance; rising behind it is the Skiddaw massif, partially topped with snow.

In the days before motorised transport, packhorse bridges such as Ashness were common particularly in upland areas where streams could easily flood during wet weather. They were designed to accommodate horses in single-file loaded with side-bags so there is often very little room for modern vehicles. Continue up the road to Surprise View and you will be rewarded with a superb vista covering the whole length of Derwent Water.

St Kentigern

The parish church of St Kentigern is located at Crosthwaite on the western edge of Keswick. Dating from the 16th century the building is the oldest in the town. Canon Hardwicke Drummond Rawnsley (1851-1920), the co-founder of the National Trust, was vicar here for 34 years, and there is a memorial to him in the baptistry. He is buried here and it is particularly fitting that he lies at rest close to much of the countryside that he helped preserve. The poet Robert Southey, a close associate of Wordsworth, is buried near the north side of the tower. Inside the church there is also a monument to him with an inscription written by Wordsworth. The beautiful Hope Park (below) lies between Derwent Water and the town centre. It was donated to the town by Percy Hope, the son of a local bank manager.

Castlerigg Stone Circle

East of Keswick the Castlerigg Stone Circle is one of Britain's most important neolithic monuments. Dating from around 3000BC, the circle sits in a natural amphitheatre of hills, with panoramic views of the surrounding fells. It is thought that the circle originally consisted of 70 stones. Today there are 38 stones which form a rough oval, within which there is an unusual small rectangular setting of another 10 stones. Little is known about the origins of Castlerigg although many people have speculated that it may have been an astronomical observatory and a place for meeting and trading. When snow

is on the ground (below) the circle takes on an almost other-worldly air and the surrounding mountains, such as Blencathra, seem to crowd in around the stones. Castlerigg Stone Circle is sited on land owned by the National Trust. This ancient monument is maintained by English Heritage and there is free access at all times.

Borrowdale

Stretching from the head of Derwent Water south to Seathwaite, Borrowdale is walled in by steep crags on all sides. The tiny village of Grange-in-Borrowdale is near the southern end of the lake. A short distance upstream the "jaws of Borrowdale" leave just enough room for the road and river to snake through.

The low-slung twin arches of Grange Bridge (left) span the two branches of the river Derwent that flow either side of a small island, a popular spot for children to play on a summer's day. Most buildings in the area are constructed from green slate and the slate, pebbles and stones that line the riverbed give the clear water a striking blue-green translucence. The Church of the Holy Trinity in the village has an unexpected barrel-shaped ceiling, finished with an unusual saw-tooth design.

Rosthwaite

This unspoiled little village is in the Borrowdale valley, on the road from Derwent Water to the Honister Pass. Rosthwaite still has working farms and its herds of Herdwick sheep and drystone walls make this an archetypal Lakeland village. The hamlet is a popular starting point for many walks, including the one up to Watendlath. Rosthwaite has a hotel, a little shop and a cafe called The Flock Inn at Yew Tree Farm which stands in a delightful rural environment. The Borrowdale Show in mid September is held in fields adjacent to the village. It is a wonderful opportunity to watch all the traditional sports, such as fell racing, Cumberland and Westmorland wrestling (below), terrier racing and tug-of-war.

Village attractions

One of the joys of Rosthwaite are the two farms that were left by Beatrix Potter to the National Trust. Nearby is Johnny Wood, a traditional oak wood with nature trails, also owned by the National Trust. The attractive stepping stones (right) across the river Derwent can be found on the path from Rosthwaite to Grange. It is little wonder that Wainwright declared: "A fell walker based in Rosthwaite is like a king with many thrones".

IN LOVING MEMORY
OF A
SUNNY DAY
IN
BORROWDALE

Stonethwaite & Seatoller

Stonethwaite is the only side valley which breaches the great eastern wall of fells in Borrowdale. The two tiny villages of Seatoller and Stonethwaite lie close to each other on the valley floor of Borrowdale. Just to the west the road climbs sharply up the one-in-four gradient of the Honister Pass. The coast-to-coast path links the two villages. Seatoller (right) is little more than a cluster of houses around a farm, but the Yew Tree coffee house (above) makes an ideal stopover for walkers and other visitors. In the graveyard at Borrowdale Church, a simple rough-cast building, is the grave of Bob Graham, the famous fell-runner of the 1930s.

Watendlath

Situated at the end of an extremely narrow and twisting road from Derwent Water, this little hamlet is best approached on foot, either from Rosthwaite or Ashness – a route which also gives the opportunity of visiting the Lodore Falls on the way.

Watendlath is the sort of place where ducks and geese seem to have as equal a right to the road as cars. A working farm often means that sheep-shearing, dipping and gathering take place under the nose of visitors. An ancient packhorse bridge crosses Watendlath Beck soon after it leaves the tarn (above). The tarn is a great attraction for sightseers. Otherwise the hamlet principally consists of a farmhouse or two, one selling teas and another hiring out rowing boats for trout fishing. The entire area is in the ownership of the National Trust.

Buttermere

One of three connected lakes, Buttermere gives its name to the local village. Its remote valley can be reached either from the Newlands or Honister Passes. The village is located close to low-lying water meadows (left) where cows were kept, giving Buttermere its name. The view above is from the opposite, eastern end of the lake close to Gatesgarth Farm. The popular two-hour walk around the lake is an excellent introduction to the area. The village itself consists of little more than a farm and two hotels, The Bridge and the Fish Hotel. The latter became famous as the home of Mary Robinson, "The Beauty of Buttermere". Tourists would travel to the inn just to catch sight of her.

The Church of St James

The beautifully located Church of St James is perched on a rocky knoll above Buttermere village and has outstanding views of the lake and surrounding high fells. A simple carved stone memorial to Alfred Wainwright, the famous fell-walker and writer, is on one of the church window-sills and there is a view from the window across to Haystacks, his favourite mountain where his ashes are scattered. The porch has a functional yet decorative iron gate (right) showing a shepherd with his sheep. The same scene is often played out in real life just outside the church today. It is difficult not to agree with Wordsworth's view that "A man must be very unsensible who would not be touched at the sight of the chapel of Buttermere".

Crummock Water and Rannerdale

Just across the fields from Buttermere (left) is the southern end of Crummock Water. The view above shows the forbidding slopes of Melbreak which dominates the northern end of the lake. On the right – ablaze with the glow of dead bracken – is Rannerdale Knotts. The side valley of Rannerdale (right), leads away from Crummock Water and is famous for the bluebells which carpet its slopes in spring. This strategic point was the site of a battle where Norman invaders were ambushed and routed by the English.

Loweswater Valley and Crummock Water

The view (top left) looks across the Loweswater Valley to Crummock Water which is sandwiched between the mountains of Grasmoor and Melbreak. In the far distance is the distinctive profile of Great Gable.

Loweswater is a small lake which empties into Crummock Water under the gaze of Bunbank and Darling Fell. Rowing boats for fishing belonging to the National Trust can be hired at Watergate Farm, at the southern tip of the lake (above). A beautiful path leads to the south-western shore of the lake (left) and after Watergate Farm it leads through the mature native trees of Holme Wood, then past the National Trust bothy.

Braithwaite

Tucked away at the foot of the Whinlatter Pass two miles west of Keswick, Braithwaite has some of the best walking in the Lakes on its doorstep. The village is a regular starting point for the well-trodden 10-mile Coledale Round.

The spectacular backdrop of Grisedale Pike means that the village enjoys some fine views of the Skiddaw massif. Bassenthwaite Lake is only a stone's throw away.

Village attractions

The Coledale Beck adds greatly to the charm of the village, and the many bridges which cross and re-cross the beck make this an ideal spot for walkers. A miners' track leads to the head of Coledale, where mining for barytes and zinc took place until recently at Force Crag Mine. The mine buildings are still clearly visible along with the waste spoil dug out of the ground. The circular Coledale Round starts from the Royal Oak and includes the summits of Grisedale Pike, Hope Gill Head, Eel Crag, Sail, Sca Crags, Causey Pike, Outerside and Barrow. The walk takes just over six hours and can be tackled by anyone with reasonable fitness.

Lorton

Situated in the lush Vale of Lorton, four miles from Cockermouth, the village is split into two settlements, High and Low Lorton. Neither settlement has an obvious centre, but both are attractive villages for the visitor to explore.

The original Jennings Brewery was founded in Lorton in 1828 and later moved to its present site in Cockermouth. The old brewery has now become the village hall. The splendid "Wordsworth yew" in the centre of the village next to the hall is the subject of *Yew Trees* by William Wordsworth. The unusual circular smoke-house (below right) is in the grounds of Lorton Park, a private house built in the 19th century. This listed building is currently in use for the smoking of fish and hams. Lower Lorton lies close to the river Cocker and this fast-flowing stream was formerly used to power flour and linen mills.

Wythop Mill

The charming hamlet of Wythop Mill (above), originally the site of a large cornmill, is located on the south side of the A66 between Keswick and Cockermouth. The name "Wythop" is thought to derive from the "wyth" or willow trees which grew profusely in the area. The mill dates from 1327 and was originally a fulling mill where cloth was treated to remove impurities and dirt; later it became a cornmill. Near Kelsick Farm are the ruins of St Margaret's chapel which date from 1673. In 1865 a new church was built on Sale Fell. The altar cross is made from a piece of wood from the old church.

103

Bassenthwaite

The village of Bassenthwaite is located down a narrow side road one mile north-east of the lake. It nestles at the foot of Skiddaw, well away from the busy tourist centres. Apart from some tourist accommodation, Bassenthwaite gives the impression of being an ordinary village without the normal commercial features of a holiday area. This quiet unspoilt charm also extends to the neighbouring villages of Ireby and Uldale. Dash Beck rises "back o' Skiddaw" and cascades over Whitewater Dash; two miles down-stream it flows past a grassy area and playground in the village. St John's church lies close to the main road, but another parish church, the ancient church of St Bega, is set in a romantic position surrounded by fields near the lakeshore just north of Mirehouse.

Village festivals

In 1780 Bassenthwaite hosted the first Lake District regatta and sailing has continued to be popular here – the sailing club celebrated its fiftieth anniversary in 2001.

Scarecrows take over the village during the summer festival held in June each year. Locals compete to produce the most original design and at first glance it is often difficult to distinguish between the scarecrows themselves and the locals.

Close to the village, three miles north of Keswick is Mirehouse, a grand mansion built in 1666. It is rich in literary associations – it was here, in 1835, that the poet Tennyson wrote *Morte d'Arthur* which tells the story of King Arthur's sword, Excalibur, being cast into the deep waters of a lake. Perhaps the lake at Bassenthwaite was his inspiration.

Hesket Newmarket

This pretty hamlet is in the far north of the
Lake District, close to its larger neighbour,
Caldbeck. It is home to a unique cooperative
brewery and pub. Beers brewed at the Old
Crown Inn, the Hesket Newmarket pub, are
nearly all named after Lake District fells. The
one exception is Doris's 90th Birthday Ale,
dedicated to the mother-in-law of the founder.
Shares in both the pub and the brewery were
sold mainly to local people enabling the two
cooperatives to be set up and run. A logbook in
the pub records details of the "Old Crown
Round" in which walkers must reach four local
summits inside 20 hours.

The village has a wide village green with
houses on both sides. A footpath leaves the
green and leads to Watersmeet, the junction of
Cald Beck and the river Caldew. Bluebells
carpet the wooded banks in spring.

Caldbeck

This attractive village is packed with evidence of its
busy industrial and mining past. It lies on the quiet far
northern edge of the national park, 14 miles south of
Carlisle. The Cald Beck – "the cold stream" – which
gives the village its name, flows behind the church
and close to the old bridge there is an interesting well.
A pleasant walk leads downstream to Priests Mill, a
converted watermill, with craft shops and a good cafe.

Upstream is The Howk (right), containing a large
ruined bobbin mill, dramatic gorge and waterfalls.
Now peaceful and with a much reduced population,
the village was booming for centuries with many
working mills and with mining in the nearby fells.

John Peel

Caldbeck is well-known as the home of John Peel, the famous Cumbrian huntsman. His ornate gravestone in the churchyard of St Kentigern (left) draws many visitors to the village. John spent his early boyhood at Greenrigg, a small farm near Caldbeck. In 1797 he married Mary White, the daughter of a prosperous farmer who gave the couple enough land at Ruthwaite, near Ireby, to give them a comfortable income. Freed from having to earn a full-time living from farming, John developed a passion for hunting which soon began to dominate his life. The famous song which commemorates his exploits – his obsessive hunting – rapidly became popular in the locality. However his story had a less than happy ending: Peel's passion for the hunt meant he neglected his farm completely and brought serious debt upon his family. His debts were only paid off by gifts from his friends. John Peel died at the age of 78, reputedly but not surprisingly from a fall while hunting, and he was buried in the churchyard at Caldbeck in 1854.

Western Lake District

This dramatic area is often described as the "wild west", an image that is not far off the mark. The remote valley of Wasdale and the area around Wast Water are about as far removed from "civilisation" as you are likely to get almost anywhere in England. Even the villages of this region, such as Boot and Wasdale Head, appear as tiny islands in a sea of wild and untamed countryside. It is this very remoteness which attracts visitors to the area. Head towards the coast and the scenery changes completely especially around picturesque and historic towns such as St Bees and Ravenglass.

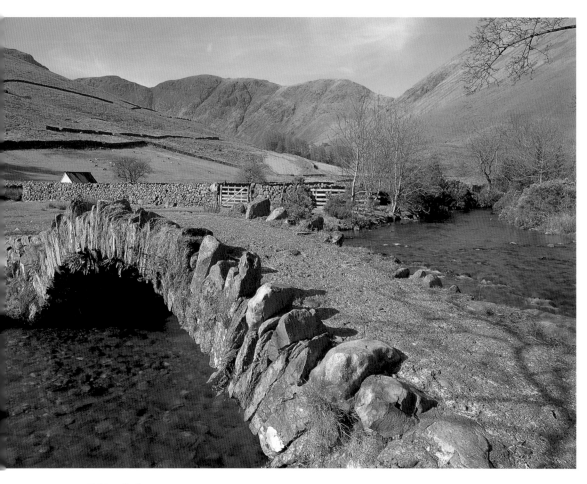

Wasdale

Close to the west coast of Cumbria, Wasdale is a hidden corner of the Lake District which, due to its remote location, has fewer visitors than other parts of the region. However, there is much for the visitor to enjoy – Wasdale is the home of Scafell Pike, England's highest mountain, its deepest lake, Wast Water and St Olaf's, its smallest church. The photograph (right) is the first view of Wast Water most visitors will see as they approach from the west. On the right can be seen the rounded slopes of Scafell with Scafell Pike behind. Directly ahead are the sheer slopes of Great Gable. The photograph above shows the packhorse bridge which lies behind the Wasdale Head Inn at the far end of the lake.

Wast Water

One of the most distinctive features of Wast Water is the Wasdale Screes which form a dramatic, mile-long wall on the south side of the lake. The overall drop amounts to nearly 2000ft (610m). The entire length of the Screes is riven by steep gullies, which offer challenging routes for the mountaineer.

Quintessentially Lakeland, the central section of this classic view (above right) is used as the logo by the Lake District National Park Authority. The grandeur of the surrounding fells is hard to beat, and it is arguably the most dramatic scene in the Lake District. From left to right the fells in view are Yewbarrow, Kirk Fell, Great Gable, Scafell and the Wasdale Screes.

This dramatic photograph (right) of Wasdale from Great Gable is taken from a vantage point close to the Westmorland Cairn, built in 1876 by two Westmorland brothers to mark what they regarded as the finest mountain viewpoint in the Lake District. It is hard to disagree. Lying a few hundred yards south, and out of sight of the summit of Great Gable, it clings to the mountain's rim above a startling drop.

Overleaf: a dramatic view of Wast Water

St Olaf's church

The two views (right) of the tiny St Olaf's church, close to the track at Wasdale Head, show the same scene at different times of the year. The church is almost entirely surrounded by ancient yews; the path leads to the start of the ascent of Great Gable. In the graveyard there are memorials to climbers, and inside a beautiful stained-glass window shows the dramatic rock formation of nearby Napes Needle, with the dedication: "I will lift up mine eyes unto the hills, from whence cometh my strength".

The village of Nether Wasdale (below) is the tiniest of settlements and lies between Gosforth, Santon Bridge and Wast Water. Its attraction lies in its wonderfully skewed ratio of buildings: one church and two pubs nearly out-number all others. The village, sometimes known as Strands, is situated at the foot of a hill with a dramatic view of Wasdale Screes in the distance.

Wasdale Head

This tiny hamlet is the only clutch of buildings for miles around. It has a magnificent setting just north-east of Wast Water in an arena of dramatic mountains which include Scafell. The Wasdale Show in early October takes place in fields adjacent to the tiny St Olaf's church. The show features Herdwick sheep and a great variety of traditional sporting events take place, including hound-trailing.

Owners keep a close eye on their dogs during the hound-trailing events at the Wasdale Show. The event is one of Cumbria's oldest and most popular sports. The dogs follow a trail made of a mixture of paraffin and oil of aniseed. The races take place over moorland, fields and fells and, as each race unfolds, many of the owners and spectators bet on the outcome adding to the air of excitement.

Eskdale

The river Esk begins its journey at Great
Moss, at the foot of Scafell Pike, and runs
past the foot of Hardknott Pass, England's
steepest road, down to the sea at
Ravenglass. The course of the river takes
it from high upland fells down into lush
green pastures. The view (above) shows
Brotherilkeld Farm and the Upper
Eskdale valley from the slopes of Harter
Fell. Some of the giants of the Lake
District's peaks can be seen at the end of
the valley – Scafell, Scafell Pike, Esk Pike,
Bowfell and Crinkle Crags.

Hardknott Fort

Just above Brotherilkeld Farm, below the
Hardknott Pass, is the dramatically sited
Roman fort of Hardknott (right).
Founded under the Emperor Hadrian,
the fort guarded the strategic Roman
road which ran from the important
harbour at Ravenglass on the coast, over
the mountains to Ambleside. The fort
has commanding views over the
mountains and down to the sea.

Boot

Three miles west of Hardknott, Boot is the last settlement up the Eskdale valley. Iron mining in the 19th century enlarged the tiny hamlet. The three-foot gauge railway, known as "La'al Ratty", was built to transport the ore seven miles down to the railway at Ravenglass. The price of iron collapsed and the mining business proved shortlived. The railway looked doomed until it was rescued by a group of enthusiasts who turned it into a major tourist attraction, renamed the Ravenglass and Eskdale Railway.

The parish church of Boot, the 12th century St Catherine's (above) is a little distance from the village across fields, with a lovely setting on the river Esk where stepping stones cross to the further bank. Eskdale Mill, the old village cornmill which dates from the 16th century, stands on the far side of the picturesque packhorse bridge over Whillans Beck. It is one of the few remaining water-driven cornmills in Britain and can usually be seen in operation. Close to the mill pond is a glorious picnic spot.

Broughton-in-Furness

On the southern tip of the national park, seven miles from Coniston, Broughton is a large village that manages successfully to tread the fine line of catering for its visitors, yet still retains the atmosphere of a local settlement. The handsome square (left) is dominated by chestnut trees which are a beautiful sight in May with their flowering "candles". In the centre of the square is a pair of stocks (right), and an obelisk. On the south side, the 17th century town hall with its seven arches, clock and weather vane, make a superb site for the local tourist information centre.

Broughton Mills (above) with its picturesque pub is a tiny hamlet in an idyllic valley two miles north of Broughton. The small but beautiful Holy Innocents Church is well worth a visit.

Ravenglass

The only coastal village within the Lake District National Park, Ravenglass is situated at a point on the estuary where the Irt, the Mite and the Esk rivers converge.

Ravenglass was originally a Roman supply port and there are significant remains of the old bath-house still standing. Today this characterful little village, with its cheerful front gardens, makes for a worthwhile trip as well as being the terminal for the "La'al Ratty" narrow gauge railway.

The magnificent Drigg Beach (right), just north of the town, was used as a training ground for D-Day mine clearance during the Second World War.

The curving estuary channel at Ravenglass provided a sheltered haven, the only natural harbour on the west coast between the river Dee in north Wales and the Solway Firth. The Romans built an important fort here in AD79, called Glannaventa, which became the second largest port in Britain. Apart from the bath-house little is left of these Roman origins, but the mosaic (above) celebrates the town's Roman maritime past.

Ravenglass attractions

Today Ravenglass consists of a short street of houses with a slipway to the beach. In the 18th century the harbour was a centre for smuggling goods such as tobacco and brandy from the Isle of Man. In the 19th century Ravenglass was given a new lease of life with the arrival of the Ravenglass and Eskdale Railway, built in 1875 to carry iron ore from the mines in Eskdale to the coast. Today visitors can ride the narrow-gauge railway and visit the railway museum in the town.

The Roman fort at Glannaventa is now the start of the Coast-to-Coast Hadrian's Wall cycle route, which hugs the Cumbrian coast as far as Carlisle before heading east along the wall.

Muncaster Castle

Just south of Ravenglass lies Muncaster Castle, which dominates the Esk Valley for miles around. Described by John Ruskin as "Heaven's Gate" the castle has been home to the Pennington family for 800 years. Dating from the 13th century, the building began life as a pele tower to deter marauding Scots and was gradually extended into a castle. In 1862, the fashionable architect Anthony Salvin was engaged to rebuild the house and he ingeniously merged the tower and castle into one. Open to the public, the castle is a treasure trove of art and antiques with an owl centre and famous gardens.

The 77 acre woodland garden contains a magnificent collection of colourful rhododendrons, camellias and azaleas which are seen at their best in spring and early summer. John Ruskin described the Terrace Walk, which offers spectacular views of the Eskdale valley, as "the gateway to paradise". Recently completed is the Meadow Vole Maze which gives an insight into the world of small mammals.

Ennerdale Water

The most westerly and remote of the lakes, Ennerdale Water (above) and its surrounding fells seem far distant from the hubbub of tourism found in many of the lakes further east. Even in the height of summmer there are few visitors. This area's remote location is accentuated by the fact that there are few main roads: access to Ennerdale is by a network of tiny lanes. Even the lake itself is unique in Lakeland by having no paved road following any shoreline. Much of the land around the lake is owned by the Forestry Commission or the National Trust.

The lake is dominated by the great cliffs of Pillar Fell, the mountain on the right of the photograph. Pillar Rock is a 500ft (892m) outcrop halfway up the summit. It was here in 1913 that the young George Mallory gained early experience ahead of his attempts to climb Everest during the inter-war years.

St Bees

A popular destination four miles south of Whitehaven, this little town with its remarkable priory, its long sandy beach and fine sandstone headland contrasts with the mountain scenery inland. On clear days the coast of Scotland and the mountains of the Isle of Man can be seen across the Irish Sea.

The Priory Church of St Bega (above) is renowned for its richly decorated Norman doorway. The priory was established by Bega, an Irish nun, who was shipwrecked here in the 9th century.

The four-mile long St Bees Head (left) is a nature reserve. The 190-mile long coast-to-coast walk starts here and ends at Robin Hood's Bay in Yorkshire.

Maryport

Situated on the Solway estuary, Maryport has a maritime history which dates back to Roman times when a fort overlooked the wide expanse of the bay. After the Romans left, the settlement was little more than a small fishing village at the mouth of the river Ellen. In 1749 local landowner Humphrey Senhouse obtained an Act of Parliament to build a new town and harbour. He named the town after his wife Mary and in 1857 the Elizabeth Dock was opened, followed in 1884 by the larger Senhouse Dock. Today Maryport is a well-preserved town with the cobbled Fleming Square, surrounded by Georgian and Victorian houses, at its heart.